SMART SKETCH BOOK

Oogie Art's step-by-step guide to drawing body structures in pastel.

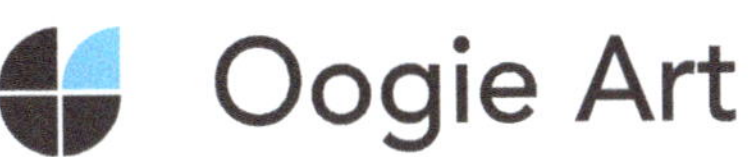

Oogie Art's SmartSketchbook™
An Expert's Guide to Upper Torso Anatomy in Pastel
First Edition, Copyright © 2015

Produced and Edited by
Oogie Art
New York, NY

© Text
Oogie Art

© Photographs
Licensed under Oogie Art®

Directed by
Wook Choi

Assistant Directed by
Clara Lu

Drawings by
Jee Hwang

Tips by
Wook Choi

Published and Distributed by
Oogie Publishing House
New York, NY
www.oogiepublishinghouse.com
(212) 714-1011

ISBN 978-0-9855809-8-8
Printed in the United States

CONTENTS

Introduction to Body Structure

The key to successful figure drawing is knowing the proportions of the human body. Standing straight, a person is about seven and a half heads high. The legs, at three and a half heads, are about half the body length. Keep in mind that these proportions are general guideline. Proportions are also different for children, adolescents, and races. Remember, do not follow these rules exactly and always draw what you see.

A basic knowledge of anatomy will also help you understand how skin lays over all the muscles, tendons, and bones of the body.

What you'll need

- Soft Pastel Set - we recommend the Rembrandt soft pastel set with 120 colors
- Pastel Pencils - a variety of pastel pencils for rendering details
- Pastel Paper - try a variety of different textures and smoothness to find your preference
- Paper Towels - wet and dry ones for cleaning hands and pastels
- 1 Vinyl eraser

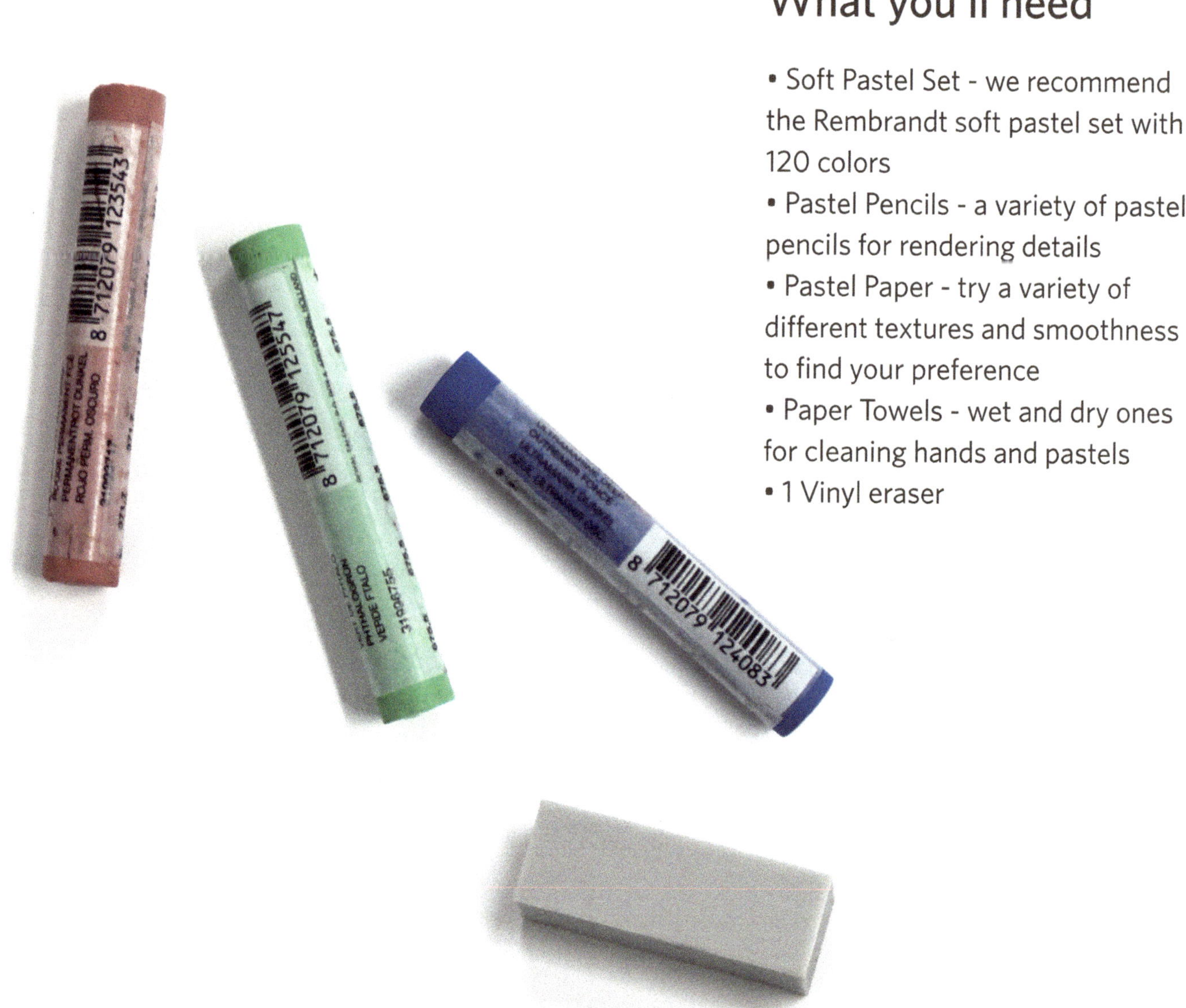

Often, the neck is a neglected part of figure drawing, drawn too small to hold up the head. The width of the neck is the same as the width of the head. The neck gradually widens as it meets the shoulders and chest. Muscles in the neck are involved in tilting, turning, and nodding, giving the head a wide range of motion.

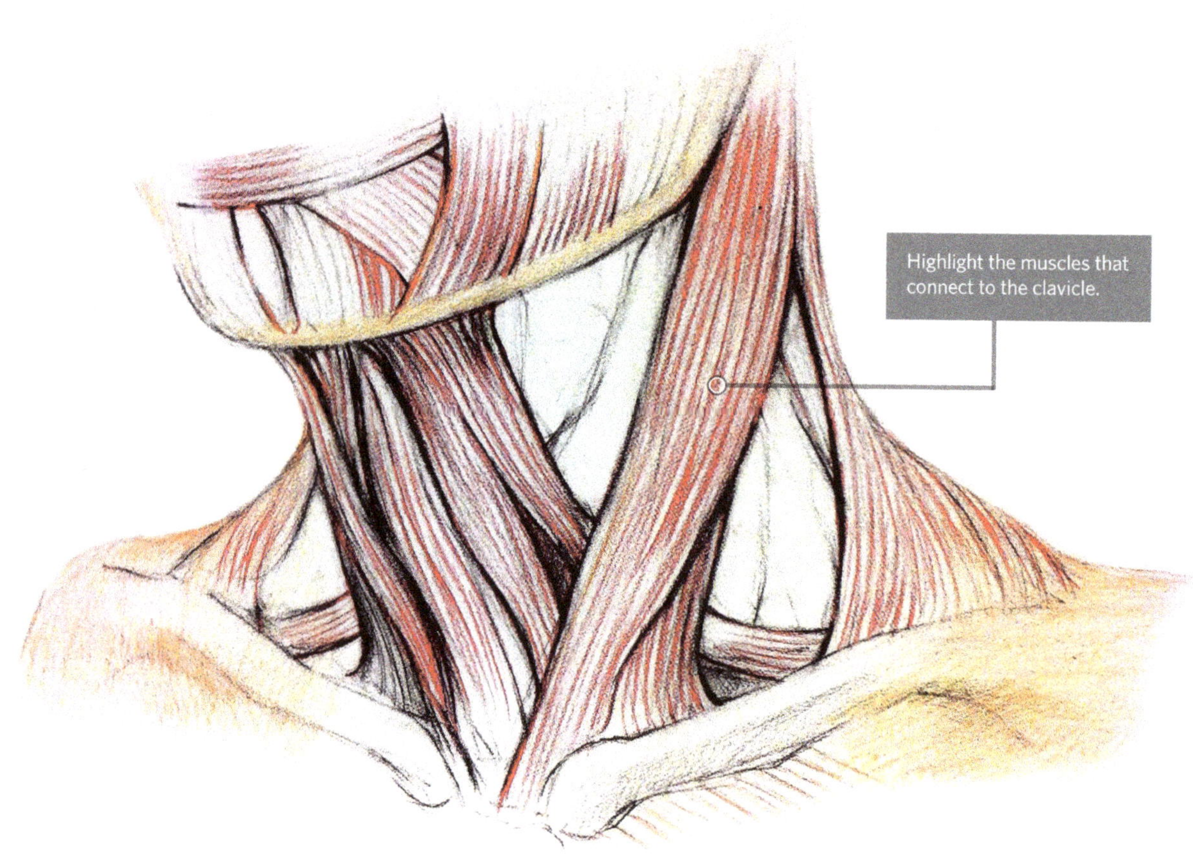

Now try drawing neck anatomy yourself.

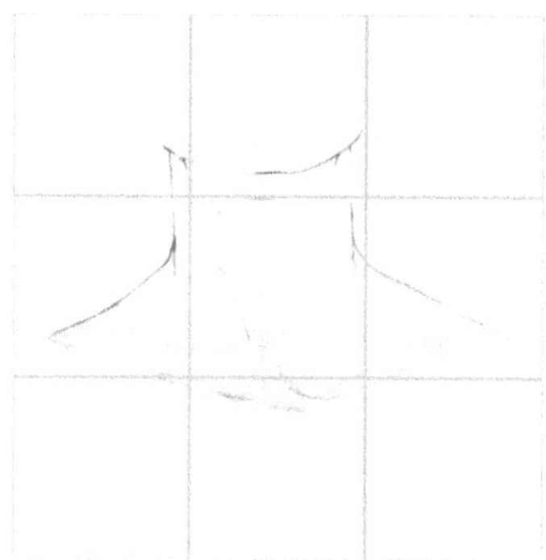

First sketch the general features of the neck area using vine charcoal.

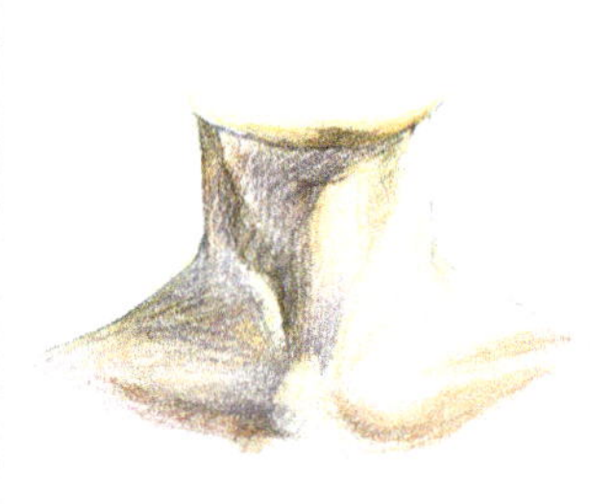

Block in the general areas of shadow and light using a light orange and yellow ochre.

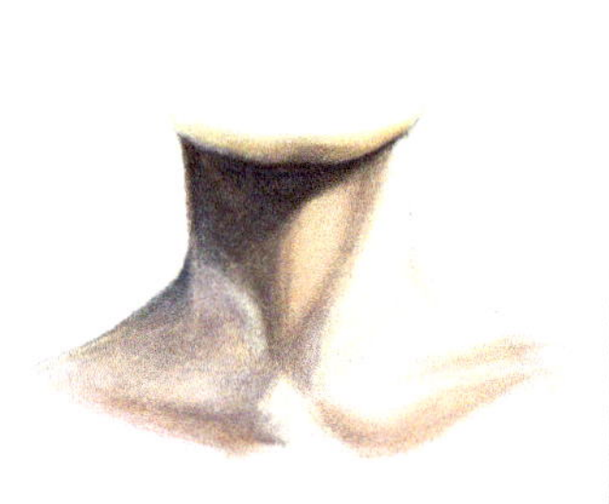

Identify the areas of light, shadow, and reflection light by layering on different light yellows, orange, light green, and pink to create rich skin tones.

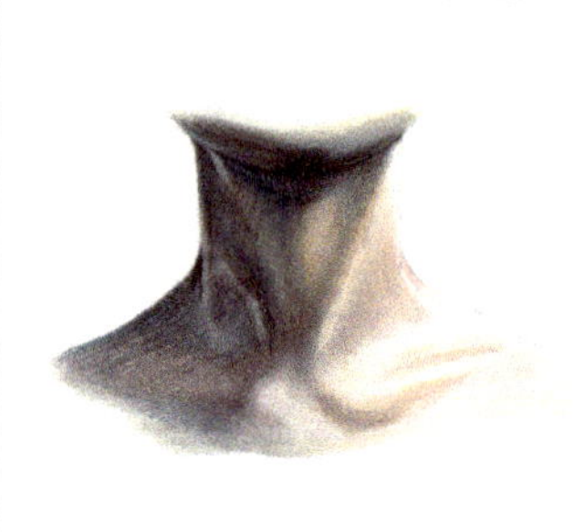

Continue to render the volume of the neck, paying attention to the subtleties in light,shadow and reflection lights. Continue to blend and add more pinks, greens and browns to create rich colors.

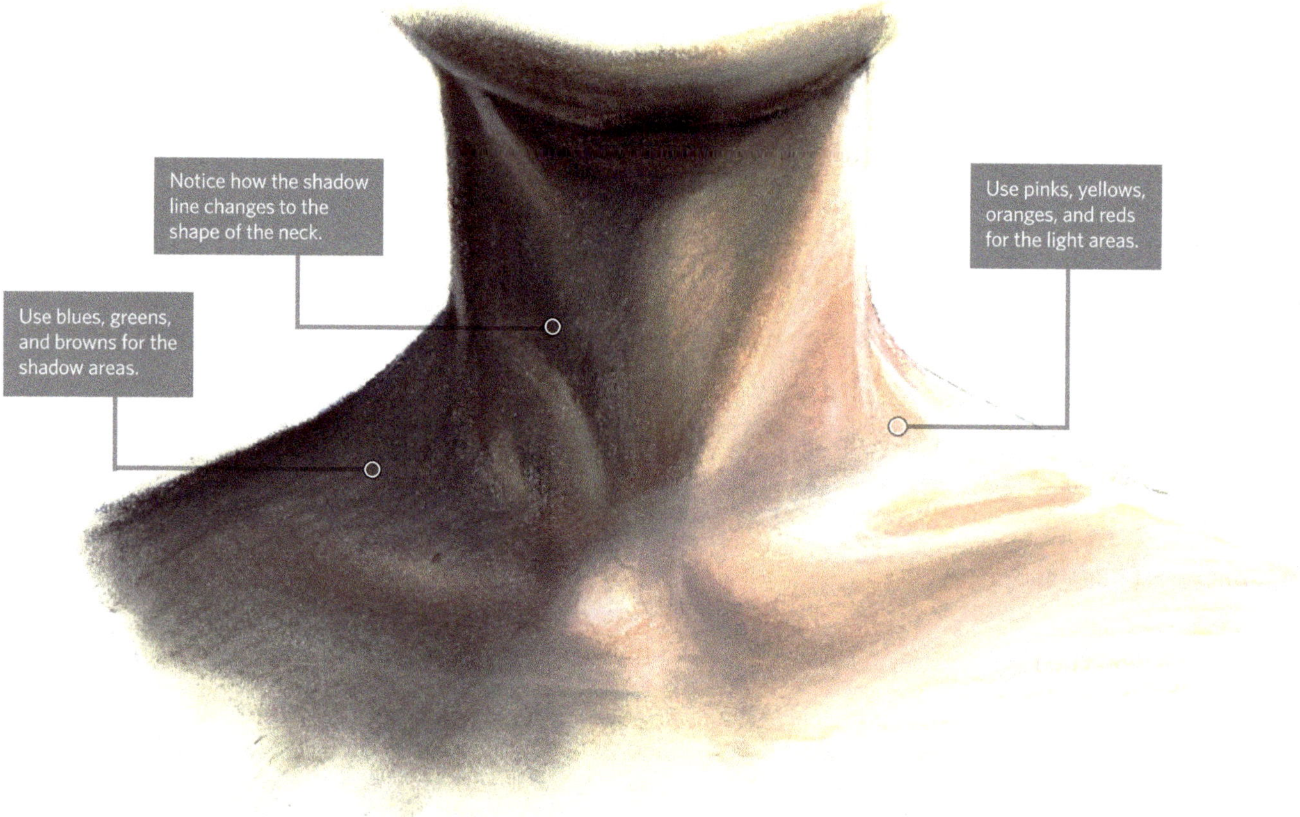

Notice how the shadow line changes to the shape of the neck.

Use blues, greens, and browns for the shadow areas.

Use pinks, yellows, oranges, and reds for the light areas.

light red oxie

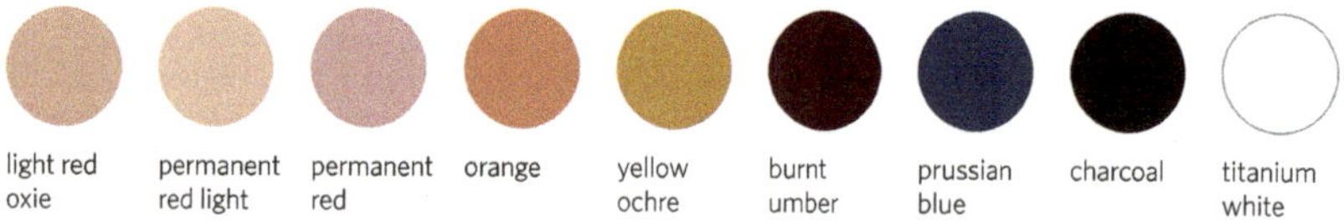

permanent red light

permanent red

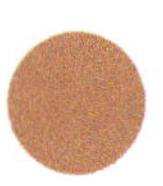
orange

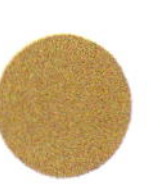
yellow ochre

burnt umber

prussian blue

charcoal

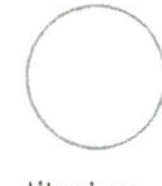
titanium white

Now try drawing the neck yourself.

Now that you have practiced how to draw a neck in pastel following a step-by-step tutorial, use the page on the right to try and draw from life. You can draw from the picture below, use a mirror, or ask a friend to sit for you and try different variations of compositions.

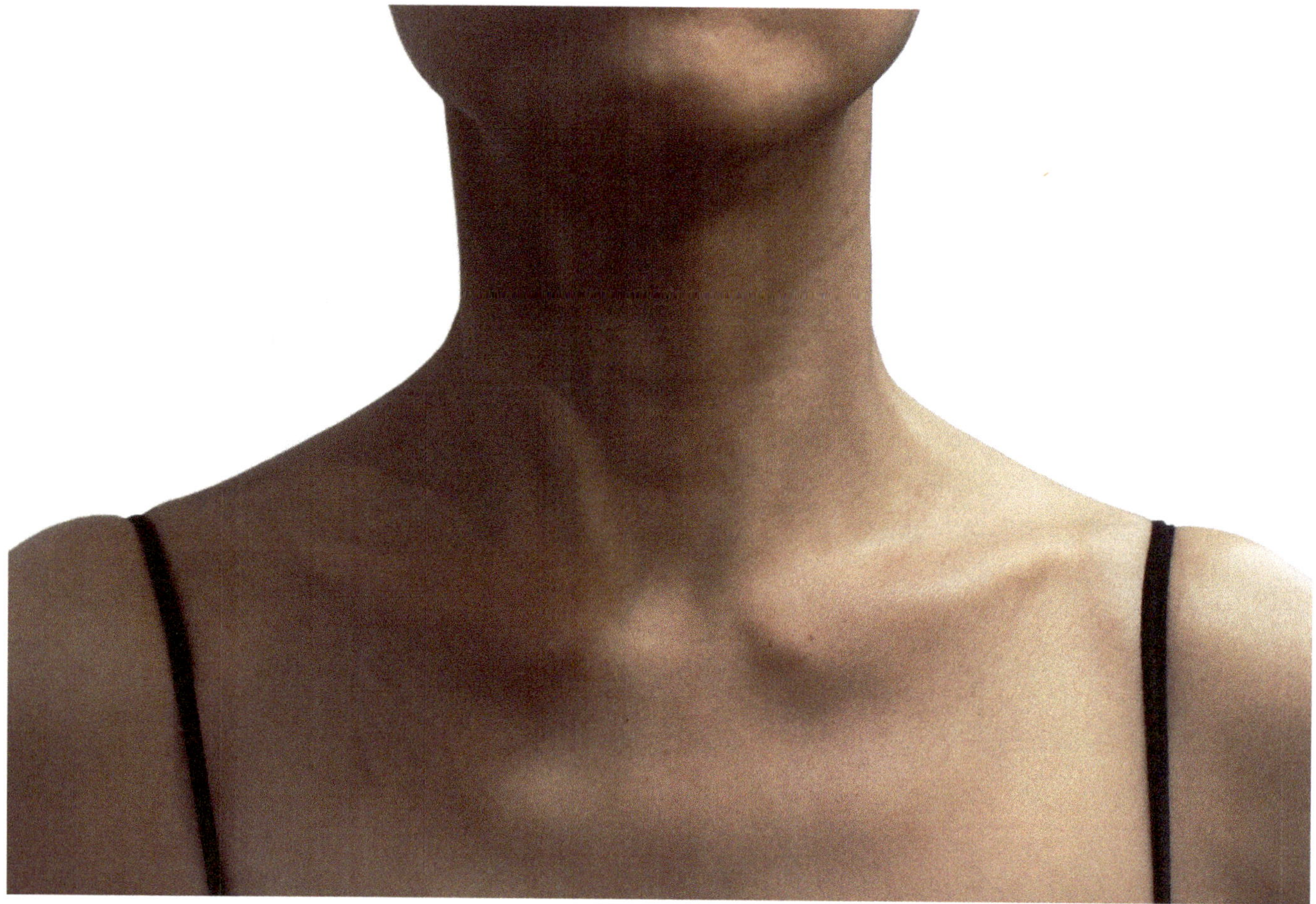

Now try drawing the neck yourself without the grid.

The torso is responsible for anchoring the base of the neck, arms, and legs. Many muscles are anchored here and are responsible for creating upper body movement. Shaped like a flattened cylinder, the position of the spine is important to drawing a successful torso.

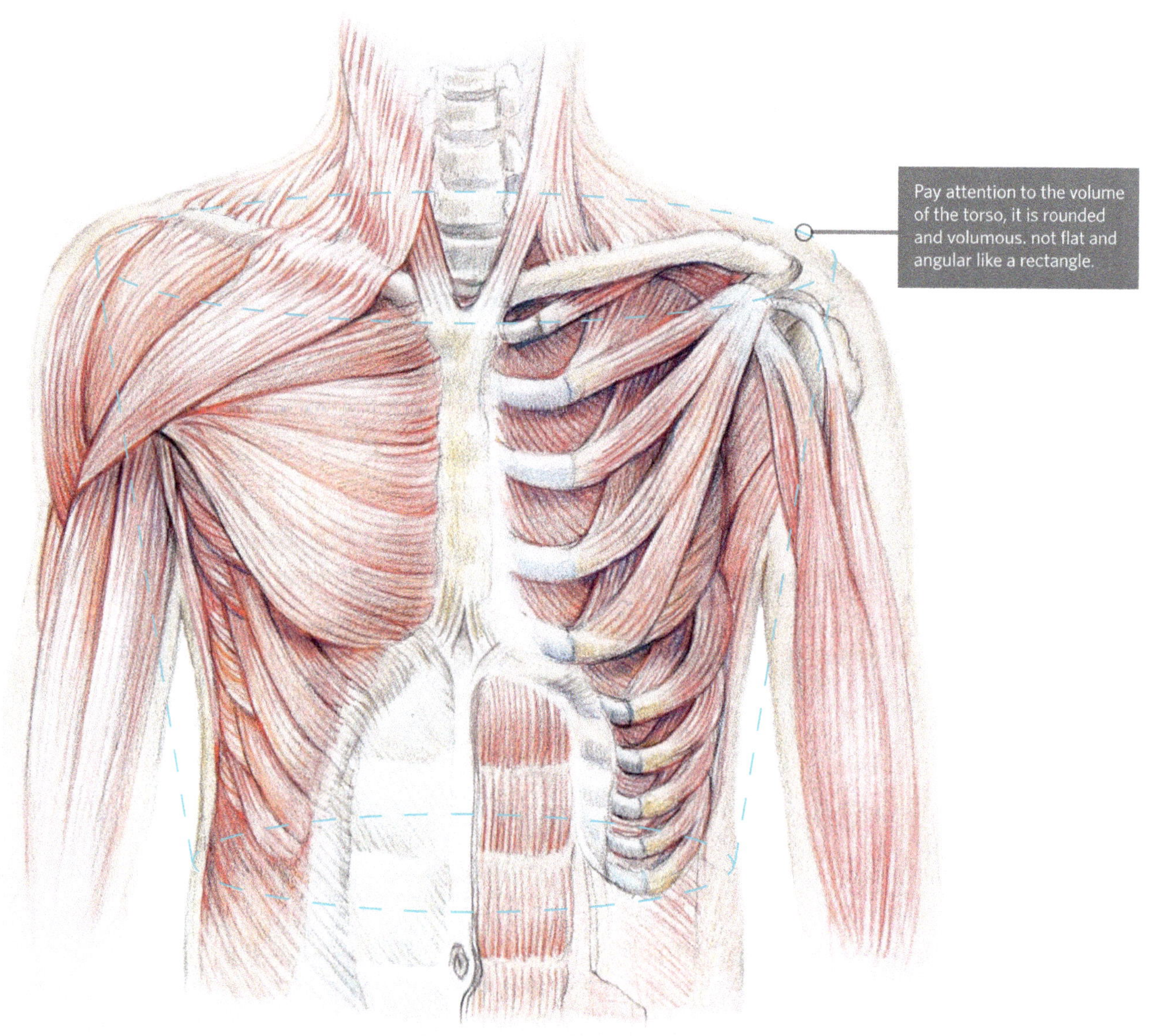

Now try drawing the neck and chest anatomy yourself.

First sketch the general features of the foot area using a light yellow pastel color.

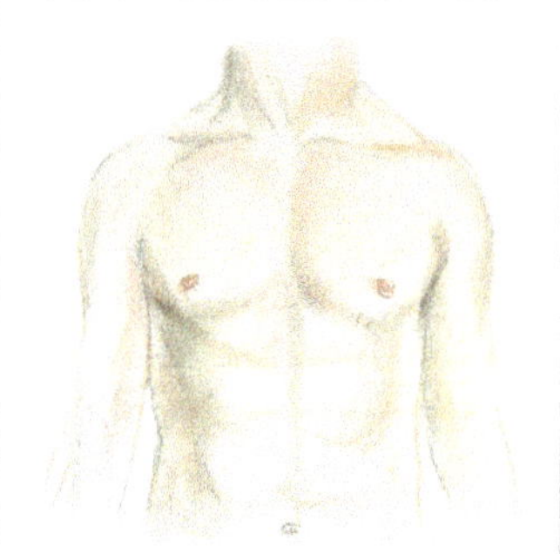

Sketch the general features of the foot area using a light yellow pastel color and connect all the shadows.

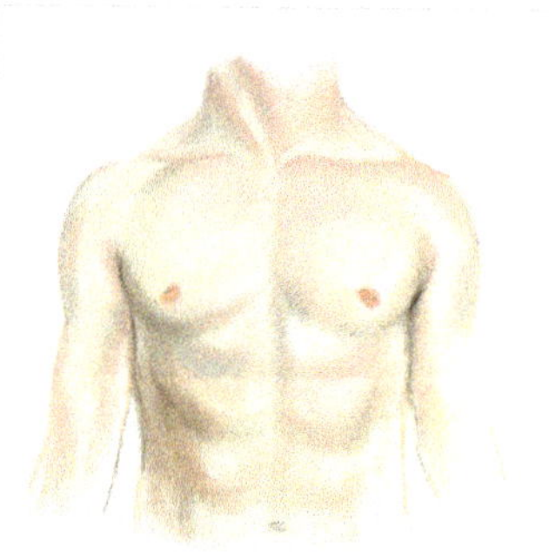

Identify the areas of light, shadow, and reflection light by layering on different light yellows, orange, light green, and pink to create rich skin tones.

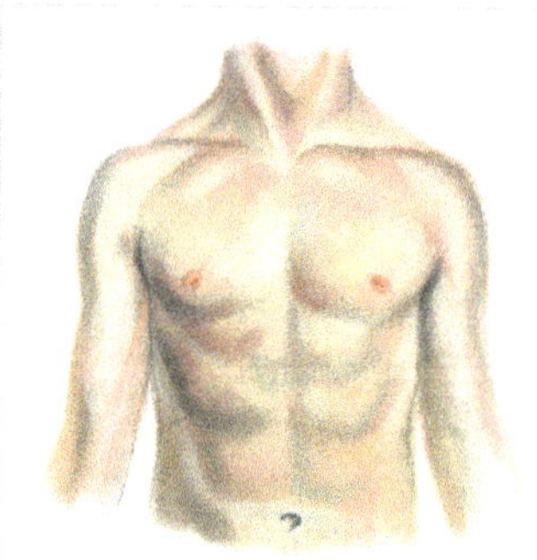

Continue to render the volume of the foot, paying attention to the subtleties in light,shadow and reflection lights. Continue to blend and add more pinks, greens and browns to create rich colors.

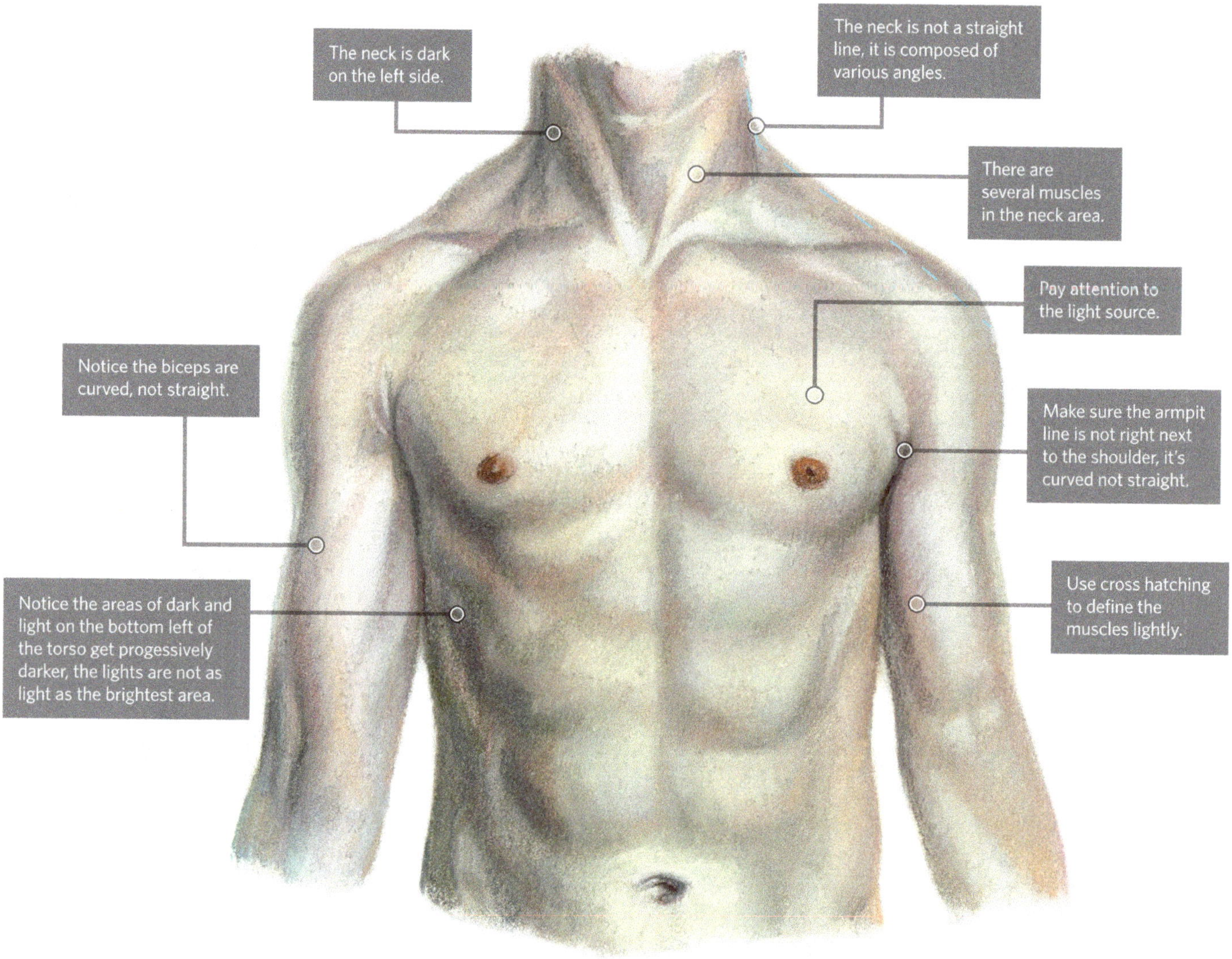

The neck is dark on the left side.

The neck is not a straight line, it is composed of various angles.

There are several muscles in the neck area.

Pay attention to the light source.

Notice the biceps are curved, not straight.

Make sure the armpit line is not right next to the shoulder, it's curved not straight.

Notice the areas of dark and light on the bottom left of the torso get progessively darker, the lights are not as light as the brightest area.

Use cross hatching to define the muscles lightly.

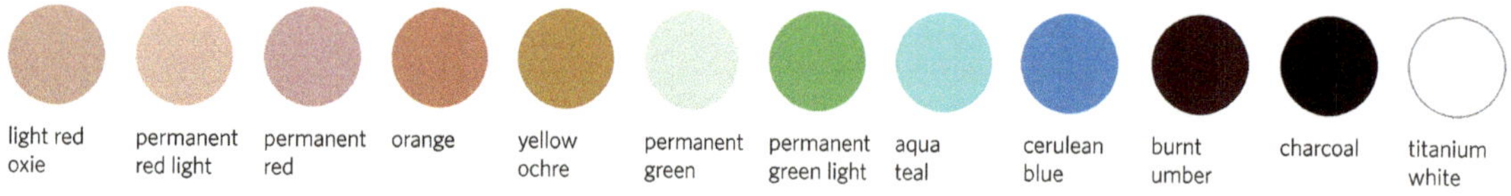

light red oxie

permanent red light

permanent red

orange

yellow ochre

permanent green

permanent green light

aqua teal

cerulean blue

burnt umber

charcoal

titanium white

Now try drawing the arms and torso yourself.

Now that you have practiced how to draw the upper torso in pastel following a step-by-step tutorial, use the page on the right to try and draw from life. You can draw from the picture below, use a mirror, or ask a friend to sit for you and try different variations of compositions.

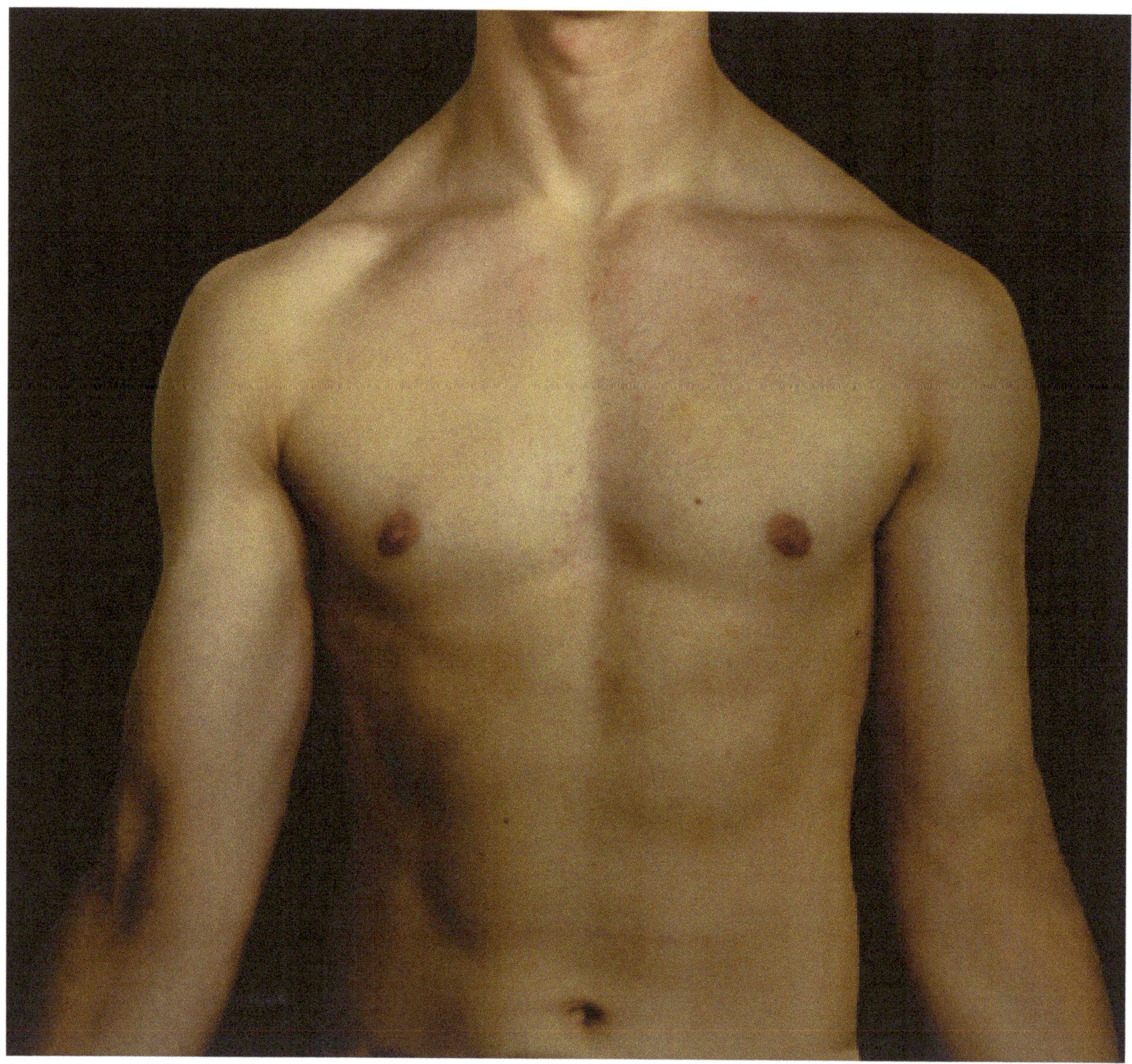

Now try drawing the arms and torso yourself without the grid.

Outline a general shape of the upper chest area using a light beige pastel.

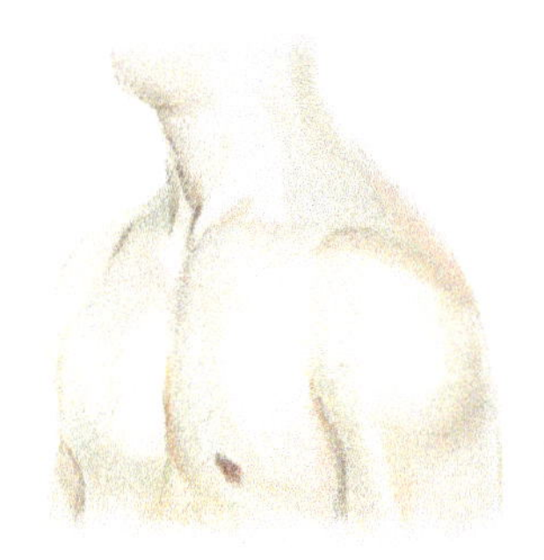

Begin to block in the general areas of shadow using light skin tones mixing in a little bit of light green, pink, and orange.

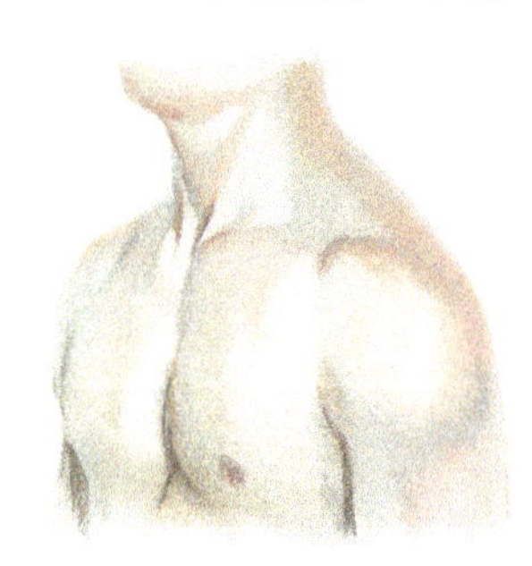

Continue to work generally and adding in darker skin tones for shadow areas. Pay attention to how the shadows are placed on the breast area.

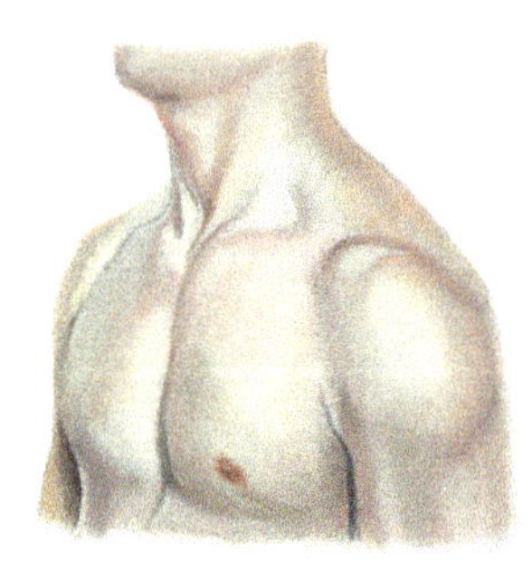

Make sure to connect all the shadows and highlights and continue building the layers of pastel.

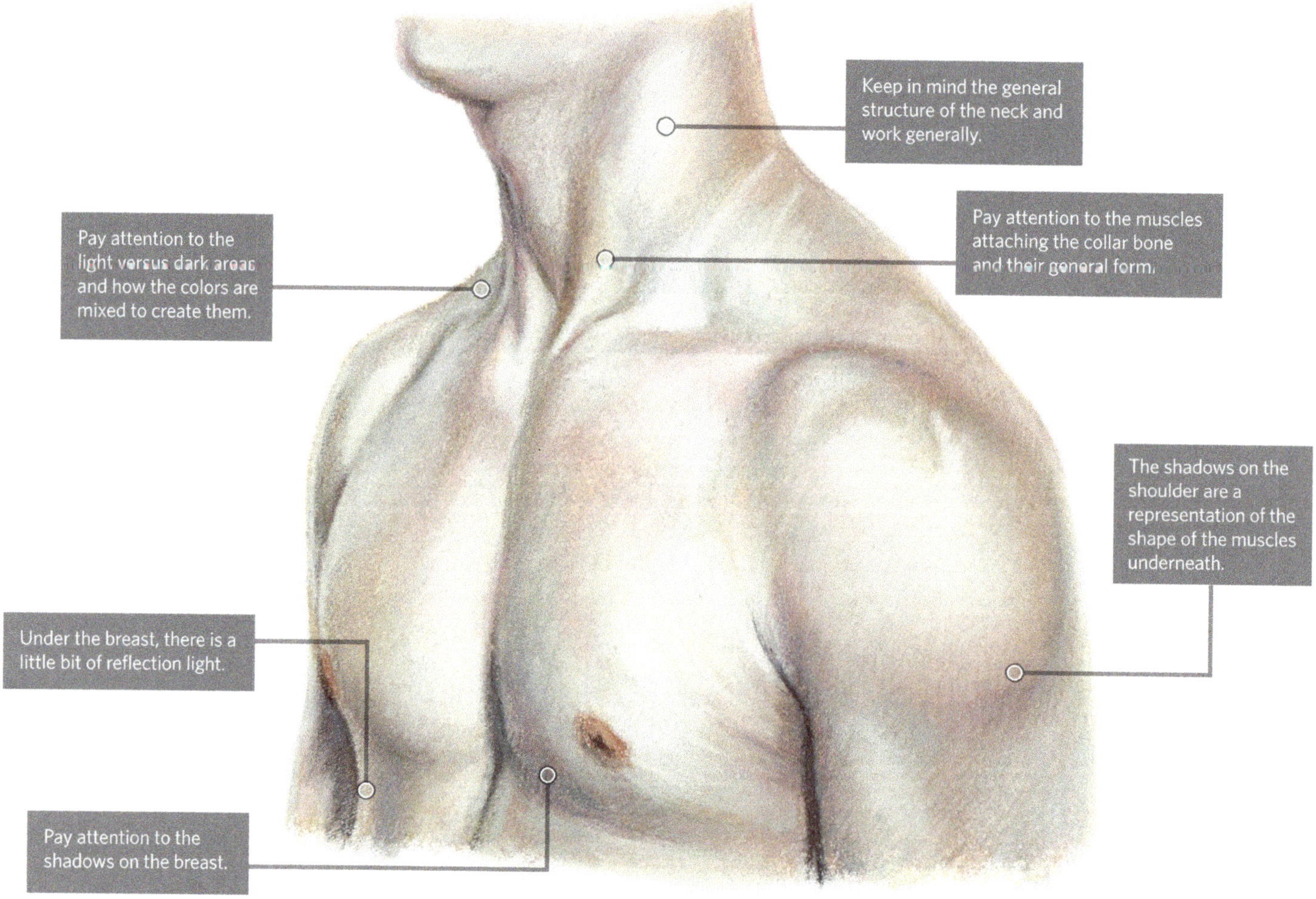

Keep in mind the general structure of the neck and work generally.

Pay attention to the light versus dark areas and how the colors are mixed to create them.

Pay attention to the muscles attaching the collar bone and their general form.

The shadows on the shoulder are a representation of the shape of the muscles underneath.

Under the breast, there is a little bit of reflection light.

Pay attention to the shadows on the breast.

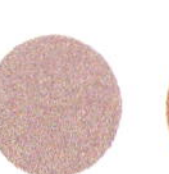
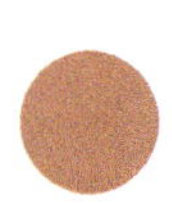
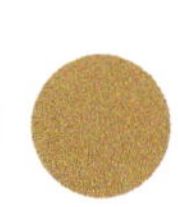

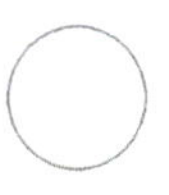

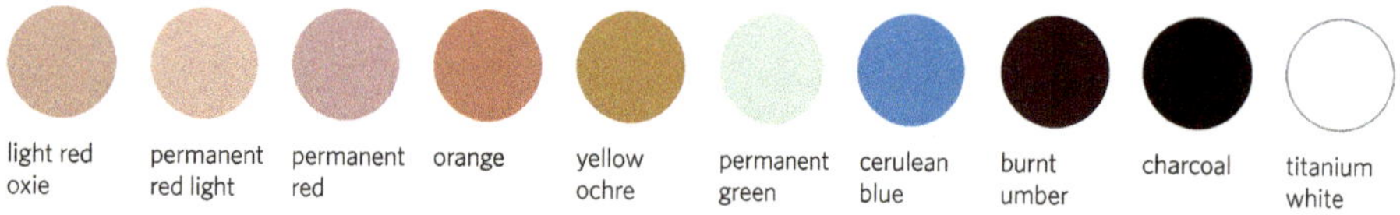

light red oxie | permanent red light | permanent red | orange | yellow ochre | permanent green | cerulean blue | burnt umber | charcoal | titanium white

Now try drawing the shoulder and chest yourself.

Now that you have practiced how to draw a 3/4 view of the shoulder and chest area in pastel following a step-by-step tutorial, use the page on the right to try and draw from life. You can draw from the picture below, use a mirror, or ask a friend to sit for you and try different variations of compositions.

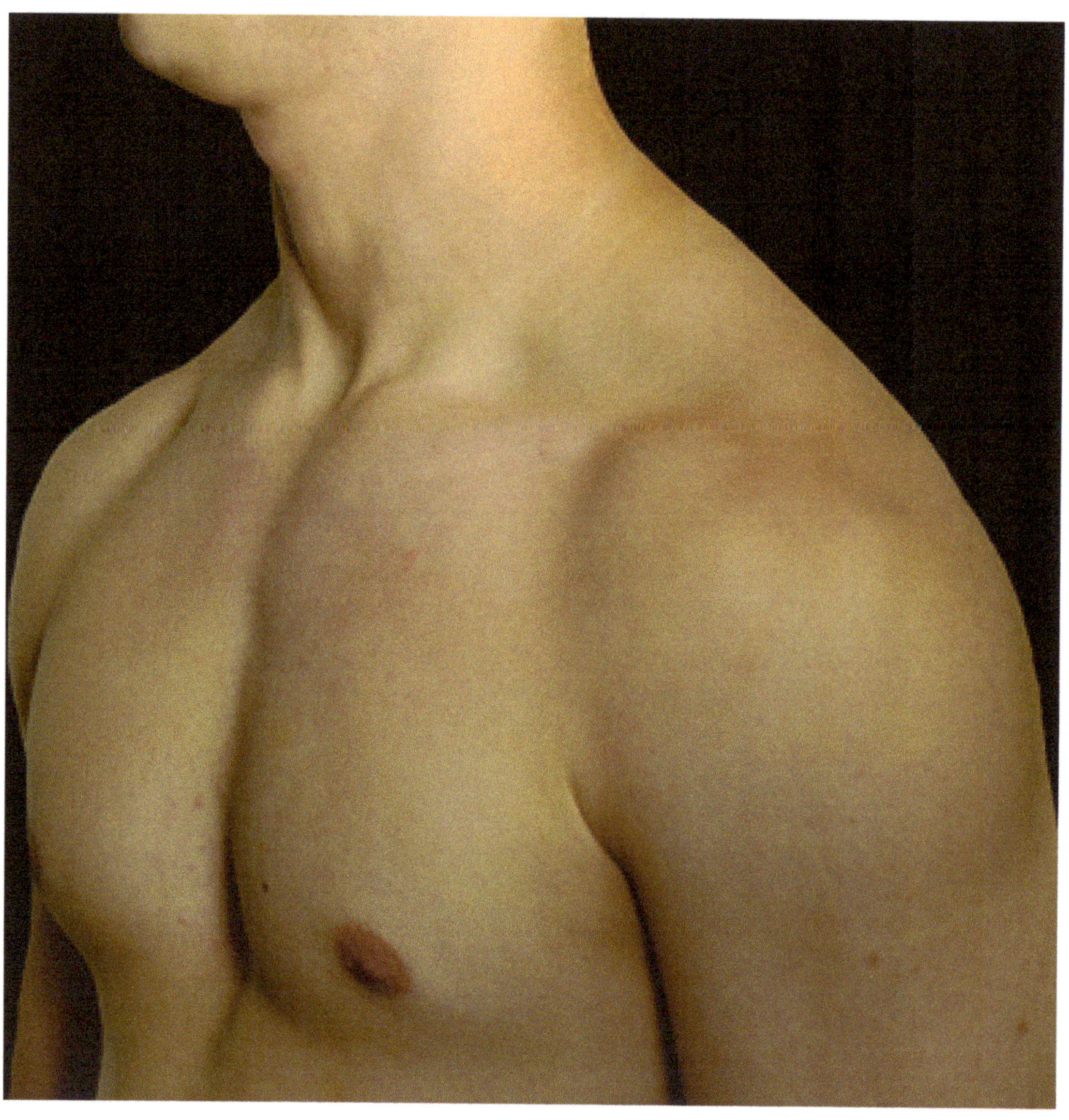

Now try drawing the 3/4 shoulder and chest without the grid.

The shoulders are the widest part of your body. They anchor the large muscles in your upper arm. The shoulder is the most flexible joint in the body, so the arms can move in a full circle. The trapezius muscles (located behind the neck and attached to the shoulder blades), creates a widening of the neck to the shoulders.

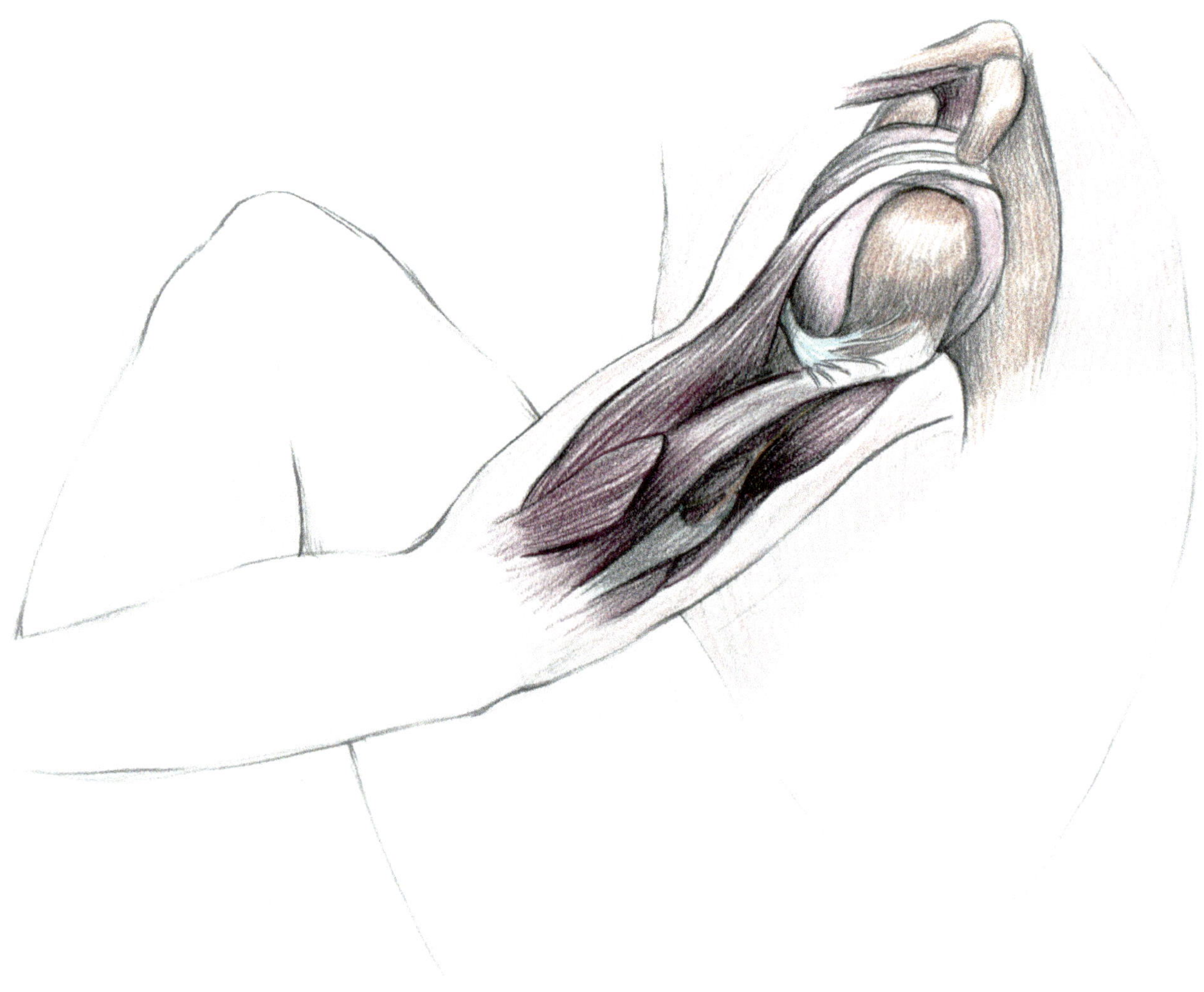

Now try drawing the shoulder and arm anatomy yourself.

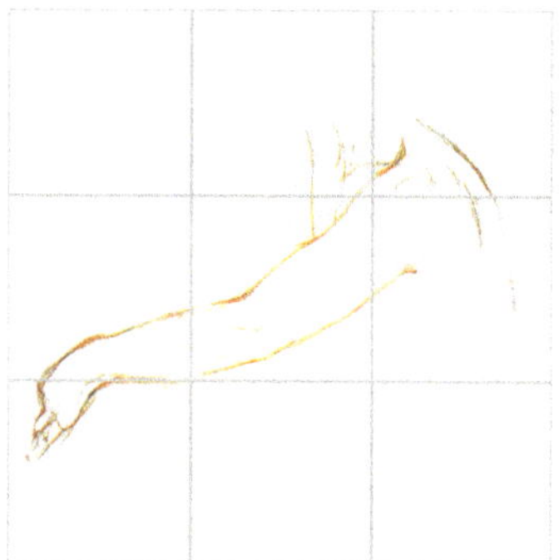

Outline a general shape of the shoulder and arm area using a light beige pastel. Keep in mind the general proportions of the arm.

Begin to block in the general areas of shadow using light skin tones mixing in a little bit of light green, pink, and orange.

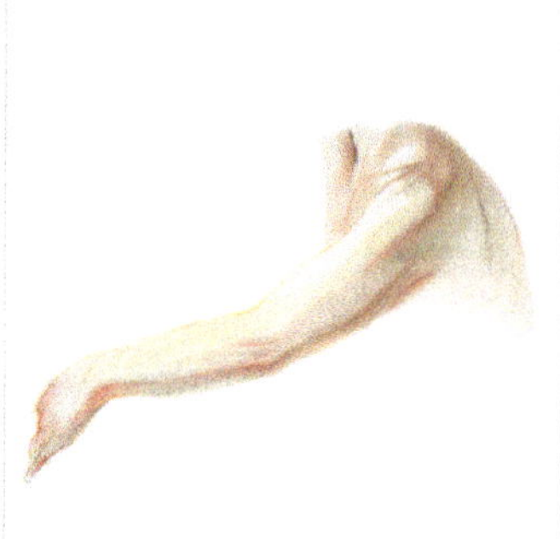

Continue to work generally and adding in darker skin tones for shadow areas. Pay attention to how the shadows are placed on the shoulder and the arm.

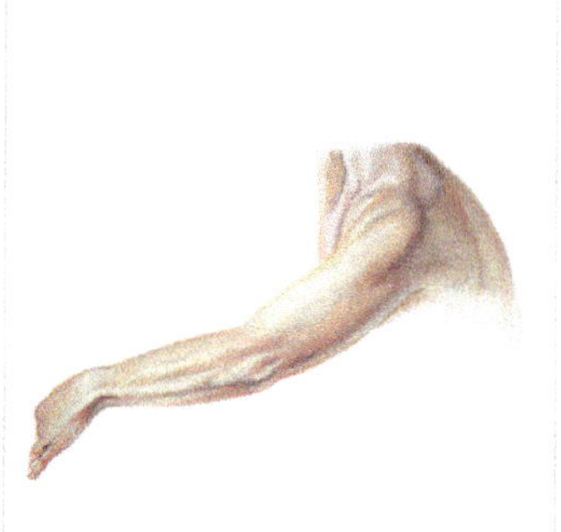

Make sure to connect all the shadows and highlights and continue building the layers of pastel.

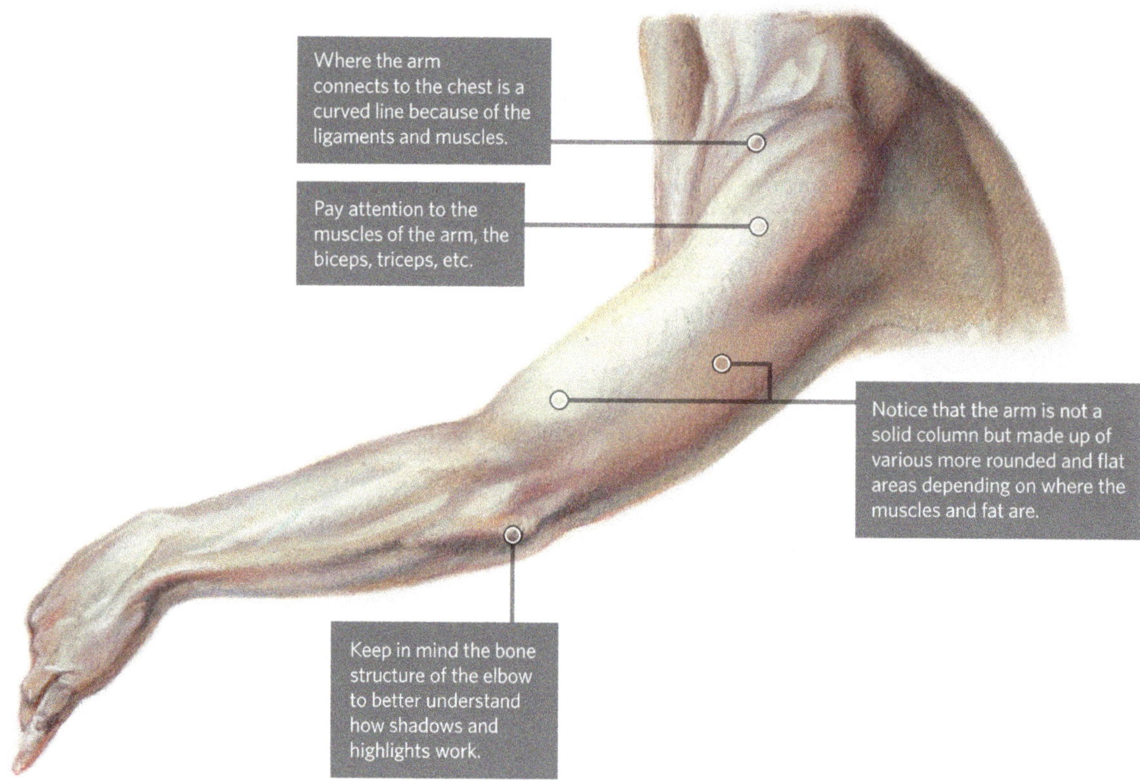

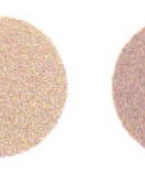

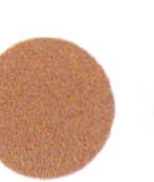
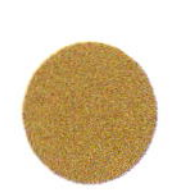
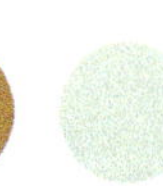

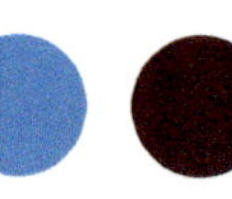

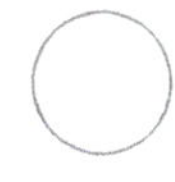

light red oxie | permanent red light | permanent red | cadmium red deep | orange | yellow ochre | permanent green | aqua teal | cerulean blue | burnt umber | titanium white

Now try drawing the shoulder and arm yourself.

Now that you have practiced how to draw the shoulder and arm area in pastel following a step-by-step tutorial, use the page on the right to try and draw from life. You can draw from the picture below, use a mirror, or ask a friend to sit for you and try different variations of compositions.

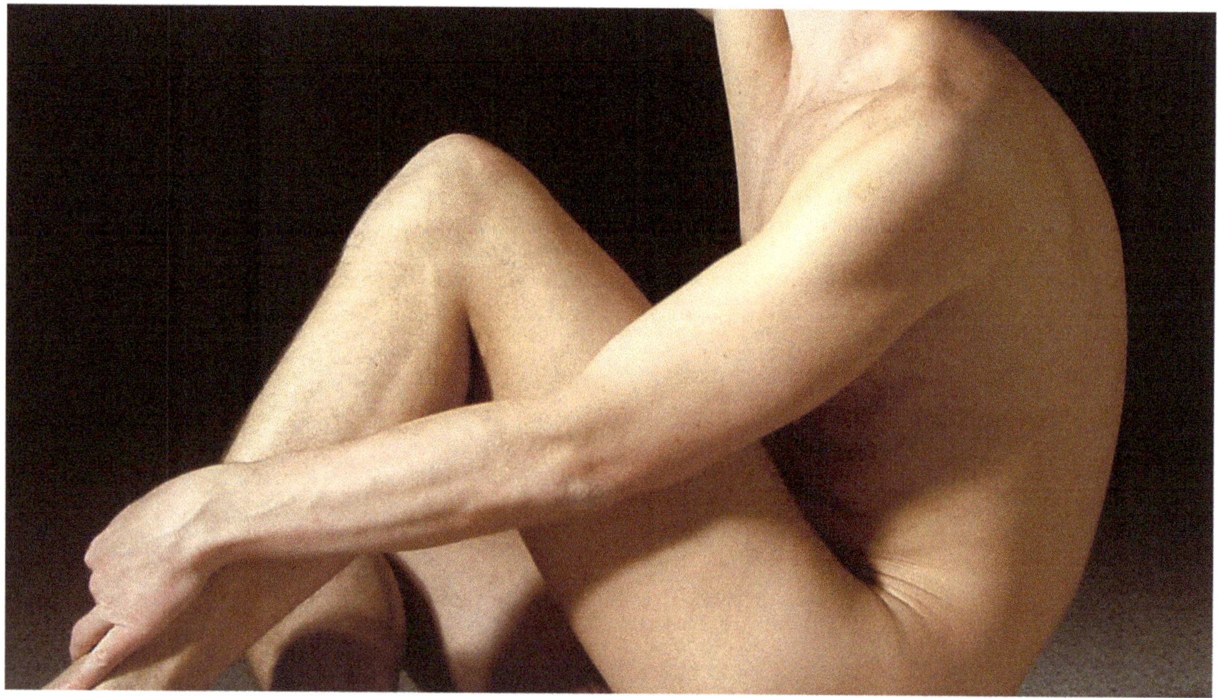

Now try drawing the shoulder and arm yourself without the grid.

The back is not just a flat plane in the body, its curves follow the curve of the spine. There are many muscles in the back as well, involved in twisting the torso as well as holding your body up. Nearly one third of the back is comprised of the shoulder blades and its muscles, the skin lays over these structures, creating bulges in the back. The waist sinks in, following the rib cage, and flares out at the hips; this is exaggerated in females while males have a straighter shape to their torso.

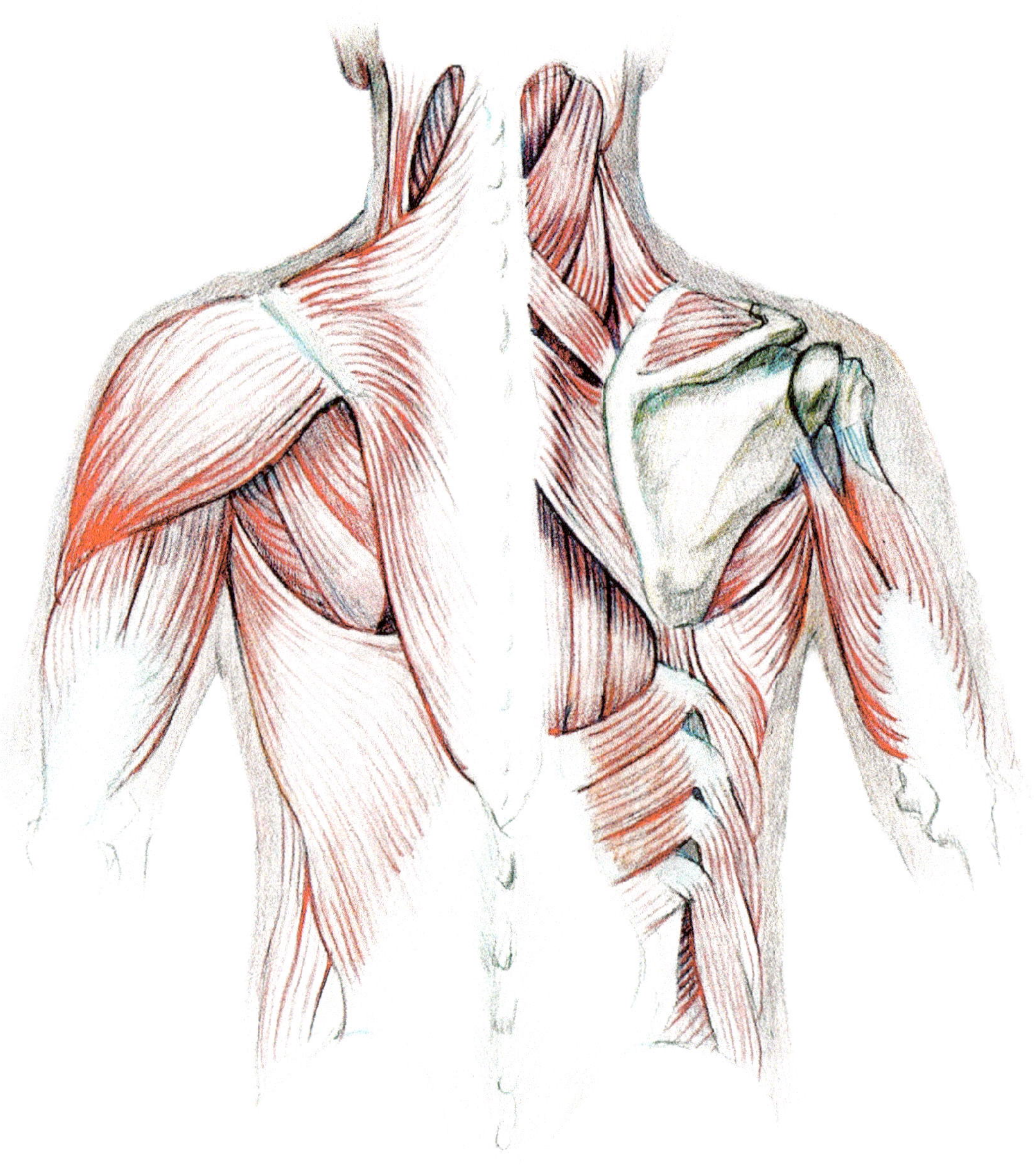

Now try drawing the back anatomy yourself.

Outline a general shape of the back area using a light beige pastel. Keep in mind the general proportions of the arm.

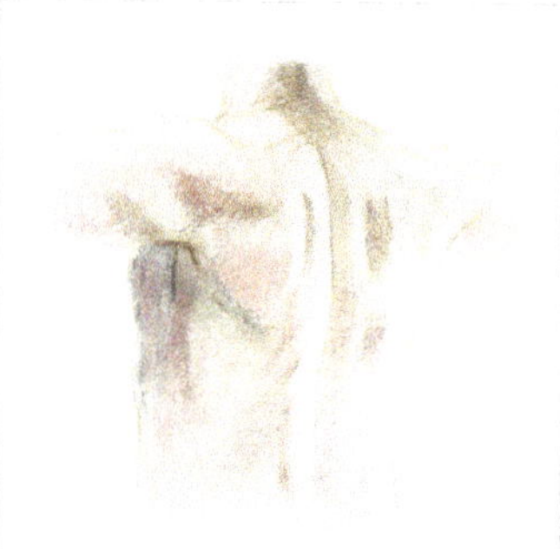

Begin to block in the general areas of shadow using light skin tones mixing in a little bit of light green, pink, and orange.

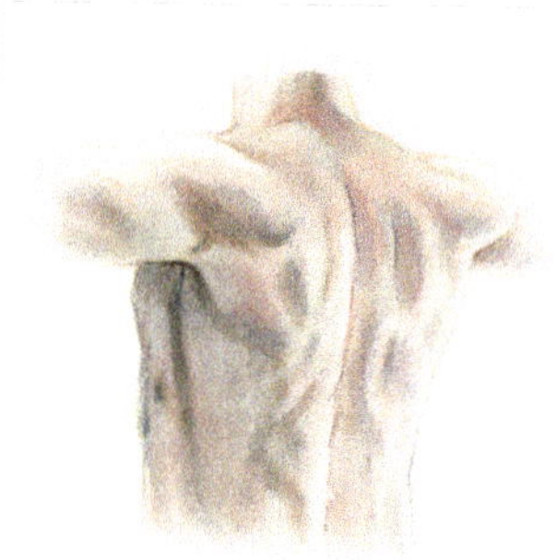

Continue to work generally and adding in darker skin tones for shadow areas. Pay attention to how the shadows affect the muscles of the back.

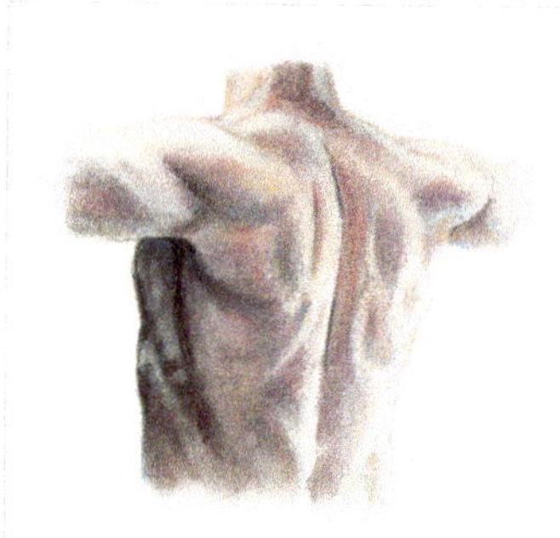

Make sure to connect all the shadows and highlights and continue building the layers of pastel.

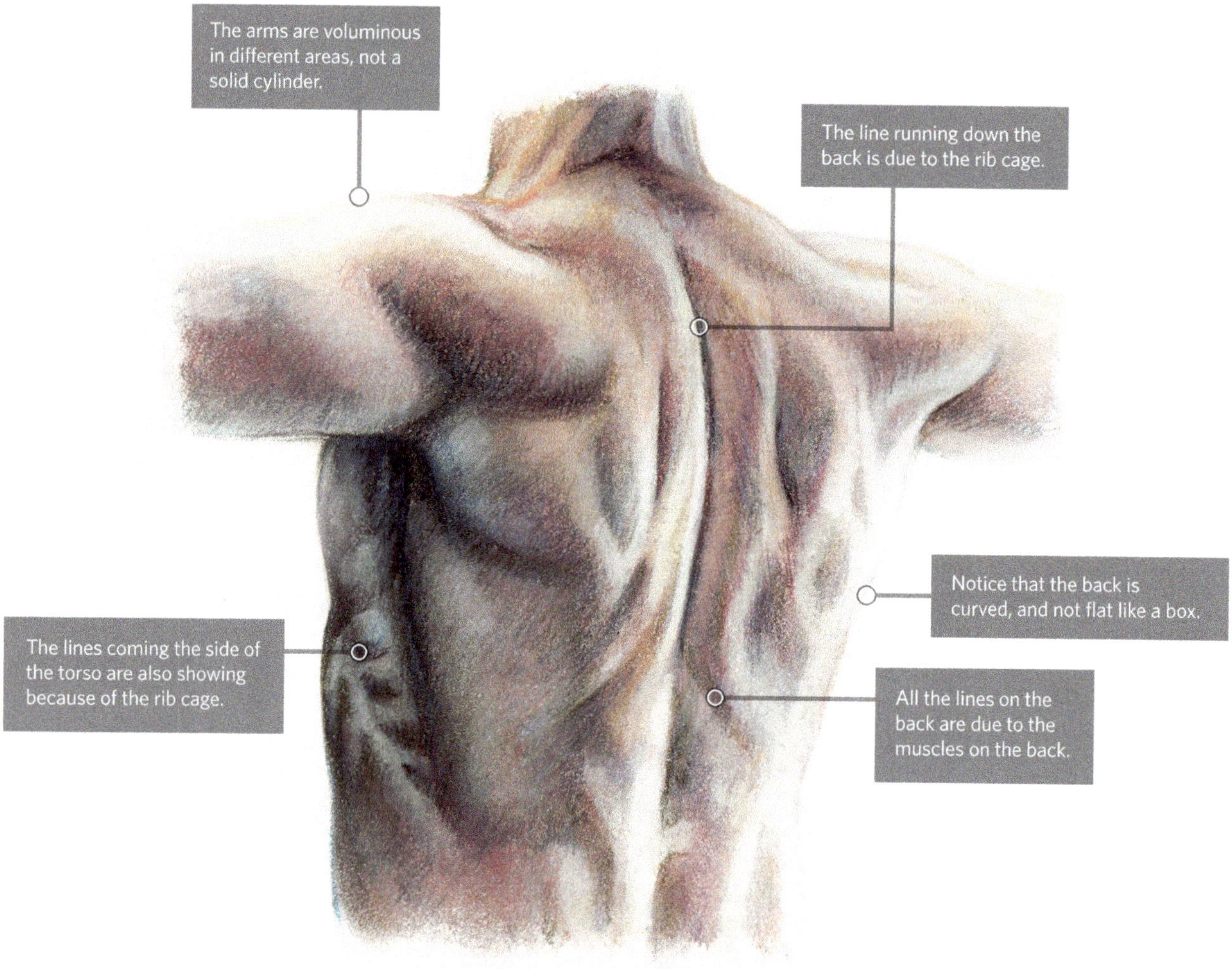

The arms are voluminous in different areas, not a solid cylinder.

The line running down the back is due to the rib cage.

Notice that the back is curved, and not flat like a box.

The lines coming the side of the torso are also showing because of the rib cage.

All the lines on the back are due to the muscles on the back.

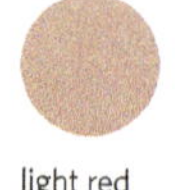

light red oxie

permanent red light

permanent red

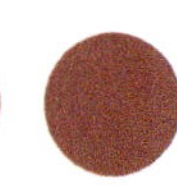

cadmium red deep

cadmium orange

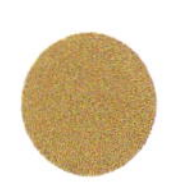

yellow ochre

permanent green

aqua teal

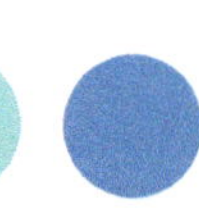

cerulean blue

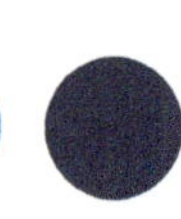

prussian blue

burnt umber

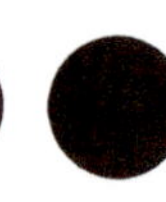

charcoal

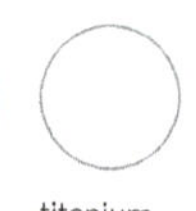

titanium white

Now try drawing the back muscles yourself.

Now that you have practiced how to draw the back upper torso area in pastel following a step-by-step tutorial, use the page on the right to try and draw from life. You can draw from the picture below, use a mirror, or ask a friend to sit for you and try different variations of compositions.

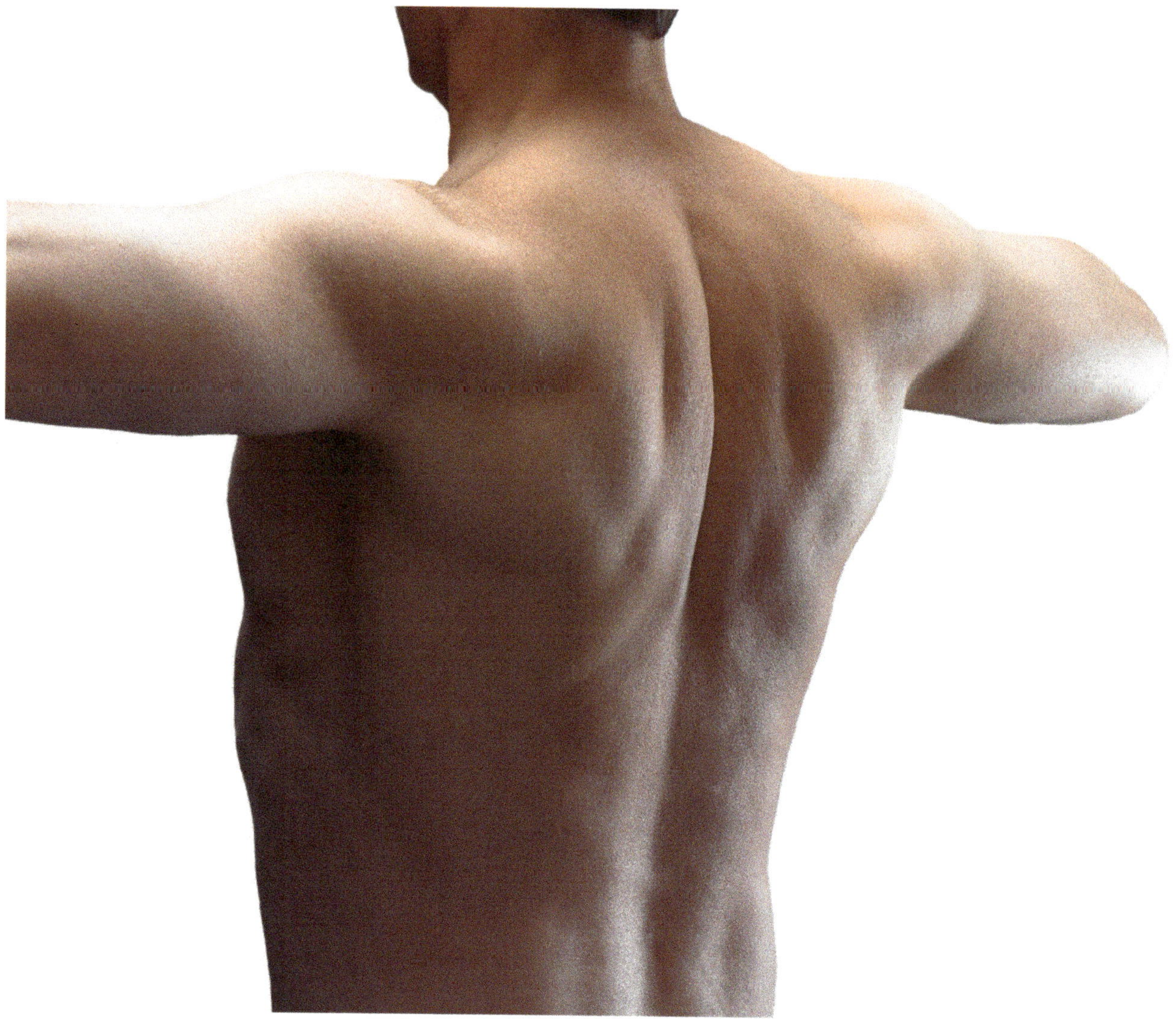

Now try drawing the back muscles yourself without the grid.

Similar to the shoulders, the hips are where the legs meet the torso. The pelvic bone that creates the hips, are about as wide as the chest, although generally, the hips are wider in females. When resting your weight on one leg, the foot lies directly beneath the head. The angle of the hips is dependent on which leg you are resting your weight. This is important in creating a realistic pose in your drawing.

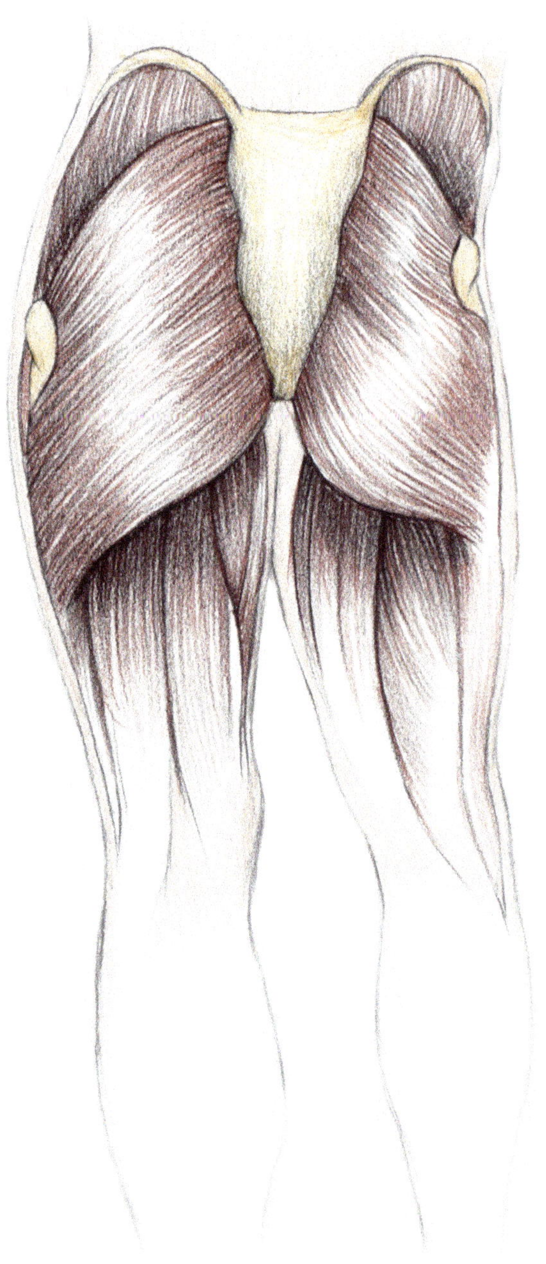

Now try drawing the hip and leg anatomy yourself.

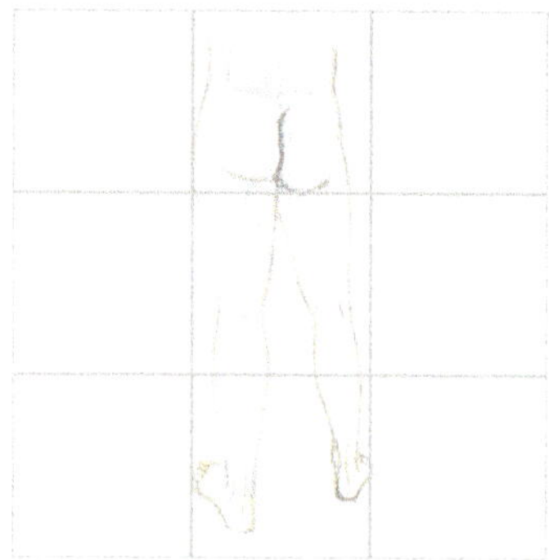

Outline a general shape of the hip and legs area using a light beige pastel. Keep in mind the general proportions of the legs.

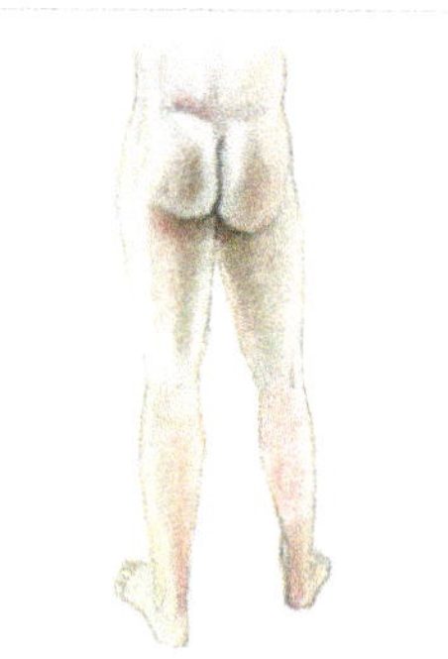

Begin to block in the general areas of shadow using light skin tones mixing in a little bit of light green, pink, and orange.

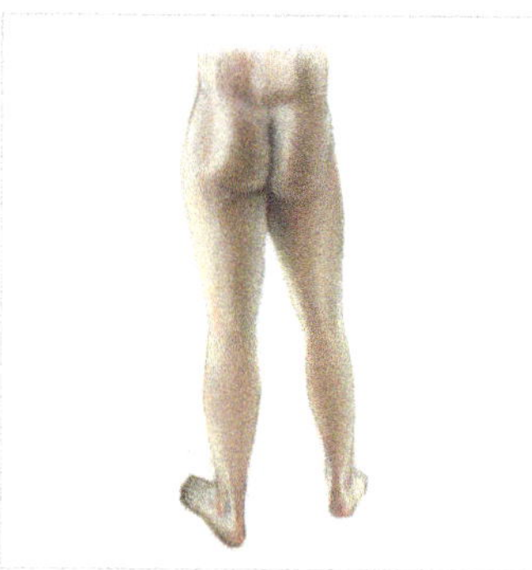

Continue to work generally and adding in darker skin tones for shadow areas. Pay attention to how the shadows affect the muscles of the butt and legs.

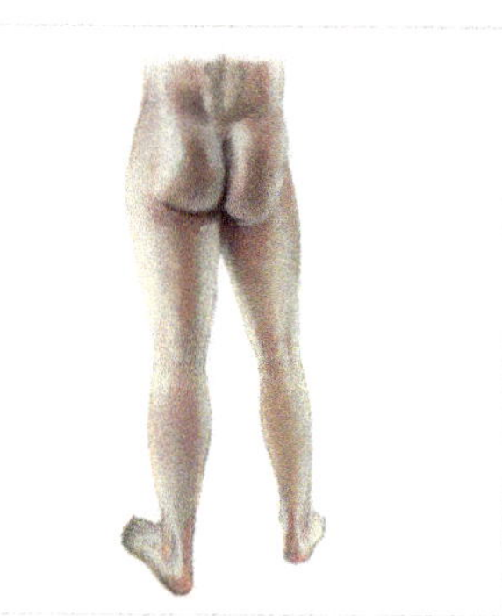

Make sure to connect all the shadows and highlights and continue building the layers of pastel.

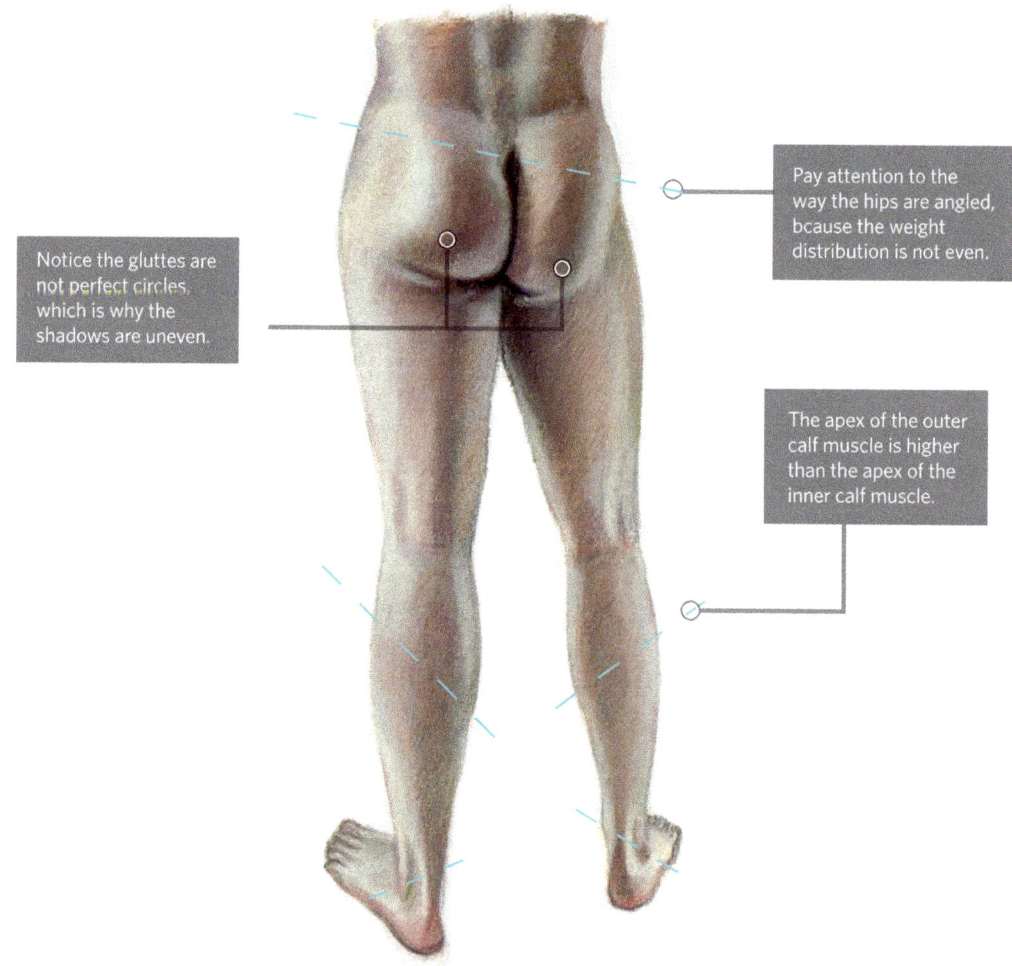

light red oxie

permanent red light

permanent red

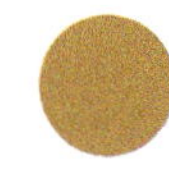
cadmium orange

yellow ochre

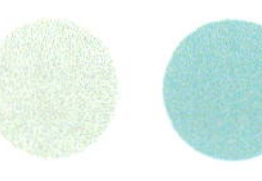
permanent green

aqua teal

prussian blue

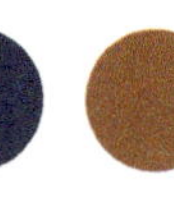
raw sienna

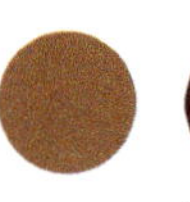
burnt umber

charcoal

titanium white

Now try drawing the hip and legs yourself.

Now that you have practiced how to draw the back hip and legs in pastel following a step-by-step tutorial, use the page on the right to try and draw from life. You can draw from the picture below, use a mirror, or ask a friend to sit for you and try different variations of compositions.

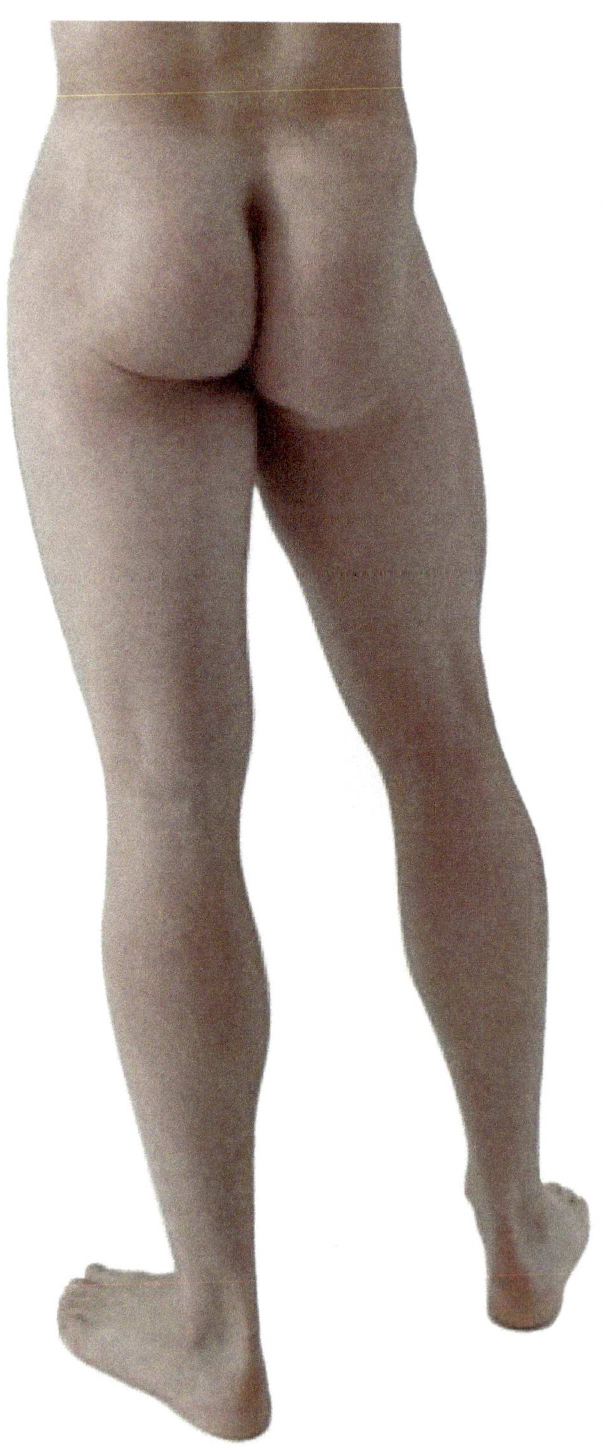

Now try drawing the hip and legs yourself without the grid.

ABOUT OOGIE HAUS

Oogie Haus is an art foundation unique for its diverse artistic endeavors, including an emphasis in art education, art & design internship opportunities, and volunteer outreach programs. There have been several book publications as well, such as "Art College Admissions," an insightful guideline for students applying to art schools.

Besides being an educational resource, Oogie Haus functions dually as an art gallery and art dealership. Through its research, it seeks to contribute a bigger network for local and international artists simultaneously curating its unique voice in todays art world. For more information please visit www.oogiehaus.com

ABOUT THE AUTHOR

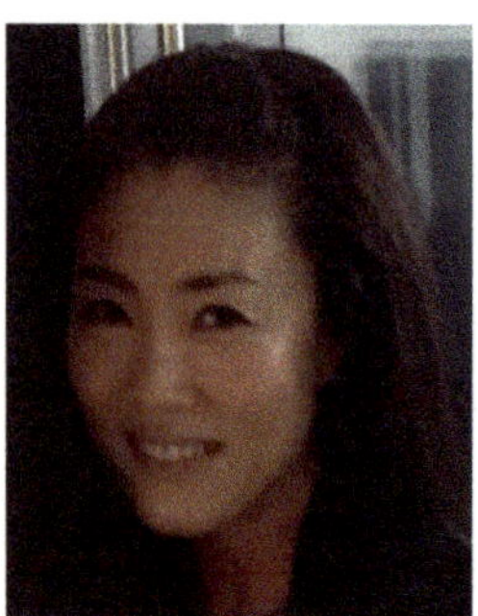

WOOK CHOI is an accomplished art dealer, education columnist, author, art educator, art gallerist, and art portfolio consultant who has guided over a thousand students to college admissions and scholarship success during the course of her 31-year teaching career.
She has received widespread recognition for her teaching methods from Mayor Michael Bloomberg; former First Lady Laura Bush; the New York Commissioner of Education, Richard P. Mills; US Congress member, Jerrold Nadler; the Alliance for Young Artists; YoungArts; and the Marie Walsh Sharpe Foundation. For more information, please visit www.wookchoi.com.

CHECK OUT SOME OF OUR OTHER BOOKS

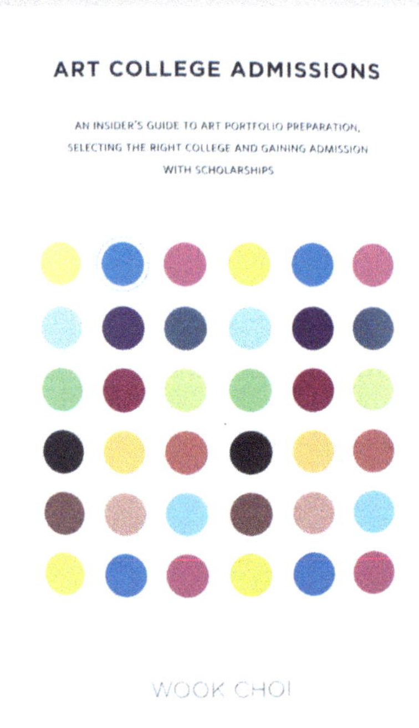

ART COLLEGE ADMISSIONS
An insider's guide to portfolio preparation, selecting the right college and gaining admission with scholarships.
In the first half of this book, you'll learn how vital a role art plays in the success of businesses today, what admissions committees at top art colleges really look for when deciding who to admit, and essential tips for developing award-winning art portfolio pieces. In the second half, you'll learn about the distinct advantages and histories of the most highly-ranked and popular art colleges in the Northeast, specific and actionable tips for getting into each school, and any changes these schools have made to their admissions criteria in recent years.

YOU CAN CONTINUE TO DEVELOP YOUR ARTISTIC SKILLS IN DIFFERENT MEDIA!

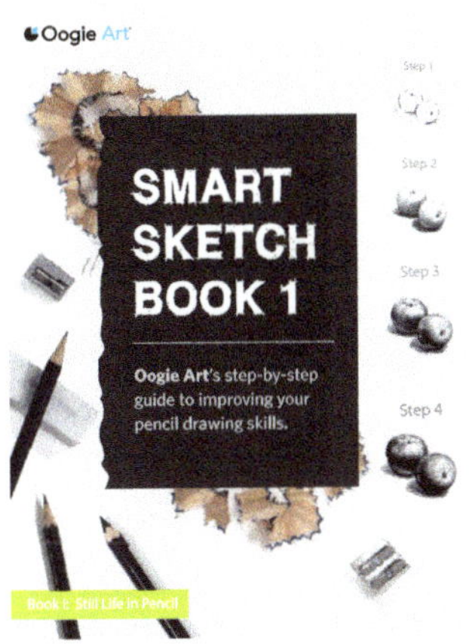

SMART SKETCHBOOK 1:
Still Life in Pencil

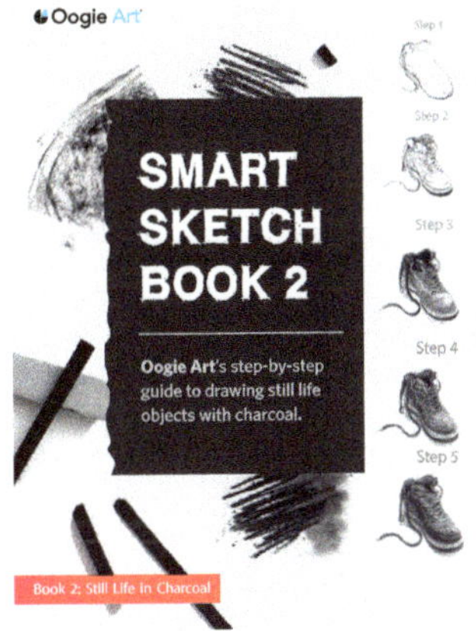

SMART SKETCHBOOK 2:
Still Life in Charcoal

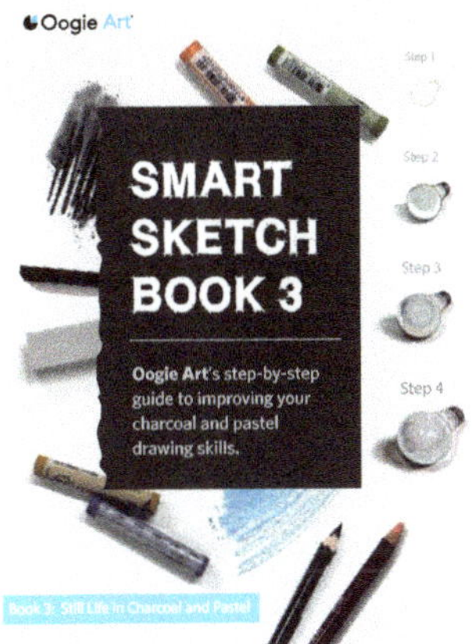

SMART SKETCHBOOK 3:
Still Life in Charcoal and Pastel

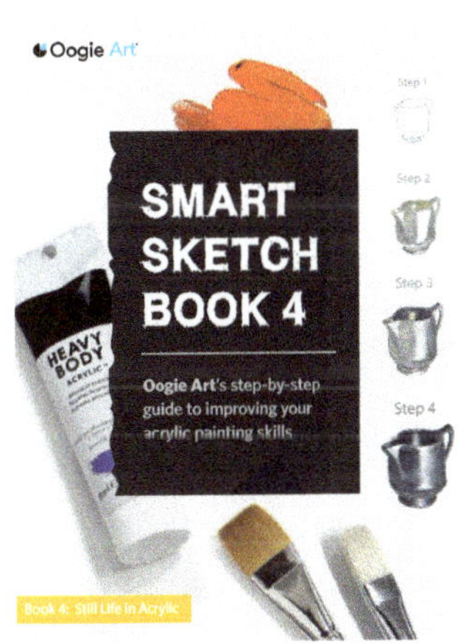

SMART SKETCHBOOK 4:
Still Life in Acrylic

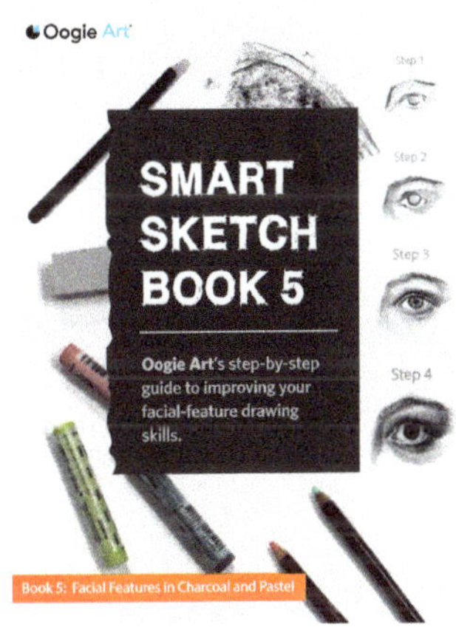

SMART SKETCHBOOK 5:
Facial Features in Charcoal and Pastel

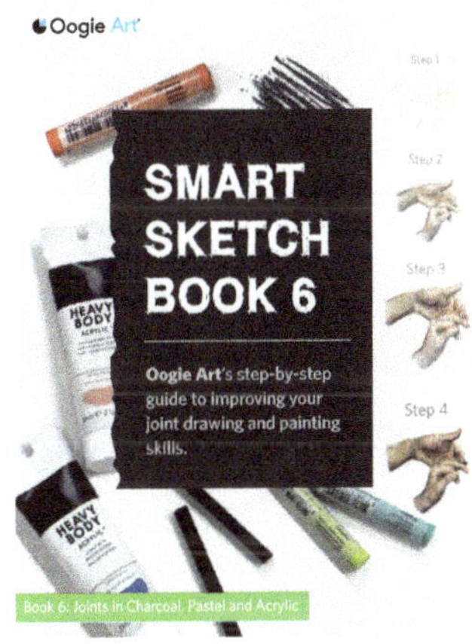

SMART SKETCHBOOK 6:
Joints in Charcoal, Pastel and Acrylic

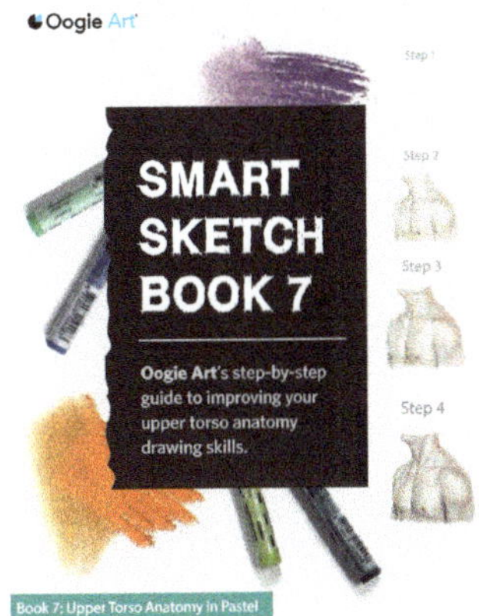

SMART SKETCHBOOK 7:
Upper Torso Anatomy in Pastel

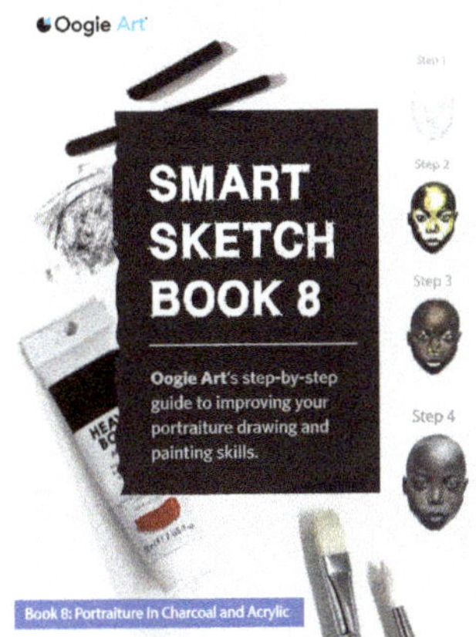

SMART SKETCHBOOK 8:
Portraiture in Charcoal and Acrylic

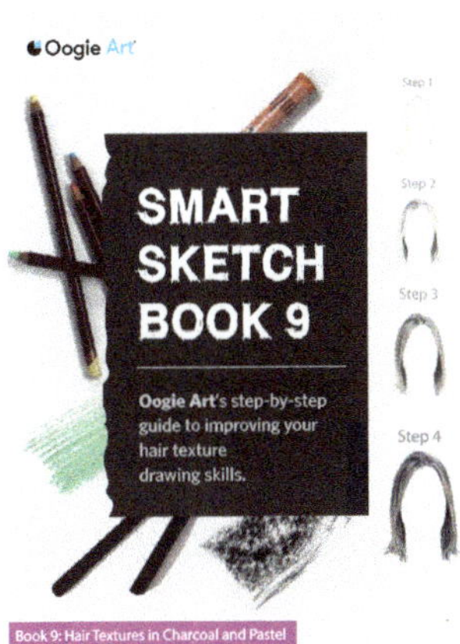

SMART SKETCHBOOK 9:
Hair Textures in Charcoal and Pastel

www.ingramcontent.com/pod-product-compliance
Ingram Content Group UK Ltd.
Pitfield, Milton Keynes, MK11 3LW, UK
UKHW062010290726
14090UKWH00022B/1488

9 780985 580988